I0409736

COUNTERING EXTREMISM AND THE THREAT OF ISIS IN SOUTHEAST ASIA

HEARING

BEFORE THE

SUBCOMMITTEE ON ASIA AND THE PACIFIC

OF THE

COMMITTEE ON FOREIGN AFFAIRS
HOUSE OF REPRESENTATIVES

ONE HUNDRED FOURTEENTH CONGRESS

SECOND SESSION

APRIL 13, 2016

Serial No. 114–160

Printed for the use of the Committee on Foreign Affairs

Available via the World Wide Web: http://www.foreignaffairs.house.gov/ or
http://www.gpo.gov/fdsys/

U.S. GOVERNMENT PUBLISHING OFFICE

99–757PDF   WASHINGTON : 2016

For sale by the Superintendent of Documents, U.S. Government Publishing Office
Internet: bookstore.gpo.gov   Phone: toll free (866) 512–1800; DC area (202) 512–1800
Fax: (202) 512–2104   Mail: Stop IDCC, Washington, DC 20402–0001

COMMITTEE ON FOREIGN AFFAIRS

EDWARD R. ROYCE, California, *Chairman*

CHRISTOPHER H. SMITH, New Jersey
ILEANA ROS-LEHTINEN, Florida
DANA ROHRABACHER, California
STEVE CHABOT, Ohio
JOE WILSON, South Carolina
MICHAEL T. McCAUL, Texas
TED POE, Texas
MATT SALMON, Arizona
DARRELL E. ISSA, California
TOM MARINO, Pennsylvania
JEFF DUNCAN, South Carolina
MO BROOKS, Alabama
PAUL COOK, California
RANDY K. WEBER SR., Texas
SCOTT PERRY, Pennsylvania
RON DeSANTIS, Florida
MARK MEADOWS, North Carolina
TED S. YOHO, Florida
CURT CLAWSON, Florida
SCOTT DesJARLAIS, Tennessee
REID J. RIBBLE, Wisconsin
DAVID A. TROTT, Michigan
LEE M. ZELDIN, New York
DANIEL DONOVAN, New York

ELIOT L. ENGEL, New York
BRAD SHERMAN, California
GREGORY W. MEEKS, New York
ALBIO SIRES, New Jersey
GERALD E. CONNOLLY, Virginia
THEODORE E. DEUTCH, Florida
BRIAN HIGGINS, New York
KAREN BASS, California
WILLIAM KEATING, Massachusetts
DAVID CICILLINE, Rhode Island
ALAN GRAYSON, Florida
AMI BERA, California
ALAN S. LOWENTHAL, California
GRACE MENG, New York
LOIS FRANKEL, Florida
TULSI GABBARD, Hawaii
JOAQUIN CASTRO, Texas
ROBIN L. KELLY, Illinois
BRENDAN F. BOYLE, Pennsylvania

AMY PORTER, *Chief of Staff*   THOMAS SHEEHY, *Staff Director*
JASON STEINBAUM, *Democratic Staff Director*

————

SUBCOMMITTEE ON ASIA AND THE PACIFIC

MATT SALMON, Arizona *Chairman*

DANA ROHRABACHER, California
STEVE CHABOT, Ohio
TOM MARINO, Pennsylvania
JEFF DUNCAN, South Carolina
MO BROOKS, Alabama
SCOTT PERRY, Pennsylvania
SCOTT DesJARLAIS, Tennessee

BRAD SHERMAN, California
AMI BERA, California
TULSI GABBARD, Hawaii
ALAN S. LOWENTHAL, California
GERALD E. CONNOLLY, Virginia
GRACE MENG, New York

CONTENTS

Page

WITNESSES

Mr. W. Patrick Murphy, Deputy Assistant Secretary, Bureau of East Asia and the Pacific, U.S. Department of State 4

Marie Richards, Ph.D., Deputy Counterterrorism Coordinator for Regional and Multilateral Affairs, Bureau of Counterterrorism, U.S. Department of State 5

Ms. Gloria Steele, Senior Deputy Assistant Administrator, Bureau for Asia, U.S. Agency for International Development 16

LETTERS, STATEMENTS, ETC., SUBMITTED FOR THE HEARING

Mr. W. Patrick Murphy and Marie Richards, Ph.D.: Prepared statement 8

Ms. Gloria Steele: Prepared statement 18

APPENDIX

Hearing notice 32

Hearing minutes 33

Written responses to questions submitted for the record by members of the subcommittee 34

COUNTERING EXTREMISM AND THE THREAT OF ISIS IN SOUTHEAST ASIA

WEDNESDAY, APRIL 13, 2016

House of Representatives,
Subcommittee on Asia and the Pacific,
Committee on Foreign Affairs,
Washington, DC.

The subcommittee met, pursuant to notice, at 2 o'clock p.m., in room 2172 Rayburn House Office Building, Hon. Matt Salmon (chairman of the subcommittee) presiding.

Mr. SALMON. This subcommittee will come to order. Members present will be permitted to submit written statements to be included in the official hearing record. Without objection, the hearing record will remain open for 5 calendar days to allow statements, questions, and extraneous materials for the record, subject to the length limitation in the rules.

In recent months, violent attacks in Europe and expanding jihadist networks in Northern Africa have provided tragic and senseless reminders of the threat that terrorism and extremism pose to the world. As we discuss the global fight against the threat of terrorism, we don't first think of Southeast Asia. But this vibrant region, home to nearly 40 percent of the world's Muslim population, is also a crucial part of the global war on terror. Southeast Asia captures less U.S. media attention than other headline-grabbing flash points, but the region's efforts to combat extremism are vital to maintaining stability in some of the world's most successful Muslim majority states and ultimately to protecting the security of our homeland.

Today, we will discuss Southeast Asia's efforts to counter the threat of violent extremism, many of them successful, as well as possible opportunities for improvement. In this hearing, we will focus on the Philippines, Indonesia, and Malaysia, but Southeast Asia as a whole is at particular risk for extremist activity.

This area is home to a large Muslim population, very porous borders, and persistent governance challenges and development needs. Militant Islamic separatists and terrorists have operated in the region for decades, but the fight against such groups has yielded some successes for the United States and our partners.

The Southern Philippine Islands have long been home to active Islamist separatist and terrorist organizations. President Bush included the Philippines as part of the front lines of the global war on terror following 9/11 and launched an effort that helped the Filipinos significantly degrade these groups. These are due, in large part, to joint counterterror operations between Philippine and U.S. Armed Forces as well as close integration between our counterterrorism and development assistance.

The Aquino administration has also made significant progress toward settling Islamic separatist violence in Mindanao with the signing of the comprehensive agreement on the Bangsamoro despite the Philippine Congress' slow progress toward implementing the terms of the agreement.

Although the Philippines has enjoyed some success, it continues to feel the pain of extremist activities. Eighteen Filipino soldiers were killed earlier this week in a clash with the Abu Sayyaf Group.

Islamist militancy has similarly been a decades-long challenge for Indonesia. Indonesia has seen more than its share of domestic terrorist attacks, including the horrific Bali bombings in 2002 and several other attacks in the following years. In response, the Government of Indonesia has built up formidable counterterror capabilities in its military and its police force thanks, in part, to the considerable U.S. capacity building. It has taken great strides in countering military recruitment by marginalizing those who advocate violence and convincing the vast majority of Indonesians that such acts run counter to the teachings of Islam.

However, the Muslim majority nation of 253 million people continues to suffer tragic terrorist attacks, most recently the bomb and gunfire attack in Jakarta in January of this year. Observers credit the Indonesian Government, including the gift leadership of President Jokowi for the comparatively minor damage that the attack caused.

While Malaysia doesn't have a history of indigenous separatists or insurgencies carrying out terrorist attacks, its government has recognized the rising threat posed by global Islamic radicalism and has taken significant measures to counteract this threat. Malaysia continues to promote the moderate practice of Islam and has shifted resources to preventing militancy from taking root in its outlying provinces. Malaysia also continues to step up its counterterrorism cooperation multilaterally and bilaterally including support from ASEAN and participation in the Global Coalition to Counter ISIL.

We have got to ensure that the positive momentum in the fight against extremism in Southeast Asia is not lost. Unfortunately, these successes have been put at risk by changes in the landscape of extremism. Most concerning is the influence of Islamic State, its malicious and viral technology and the internationalization of violence that it promotes. Hundreds of Southeast Asians have joined the Islamic State's ranks in Syria and Iraq to forge new transnational links between the Islamic State and indigenous Southeast Asian extremists. The Islamic State has reached out to Southeast Asians through social media encouraging acts of violence. There is no formal Islamic State affiliate in Southeast Asia today, but there is a threat. The linkage of the Islamic State could empower militants and rekindle a broader terrorist threat in the region.

As global terror and extremism evolves, our strategy must do the same. Today, we are going to discuss how these new challenges will affect counterterror and counter violent extremism in the region.

I was just recently in Indonesia within the last couple of weeks and I met with the newly-appointed Minister of Counterterrorism, an upgrade, I guess, from being the Chief of Police. And I can tell you that this is front and center on their minds and they are very, very concerned about potential calamities in addition to the ones they have already had. But I was able to go to one of the madrasas and meet with some of the student leaders and I was really impressed with the caliber of these young people that I met and the fact that they stand with us against extreme factions with Islam.

I look forward to hearing from our distinguished panel to develop a better understanding of the administration's strategy for this crucial aspect of U.S. foreign policy and to identify further concerns that may need attention from the committee. And I would like to recognize the ranking member today, Ms. Gabbard.

Ms. GABBARD. Thank you very much, Mr. Chairman. I appreciate you and Ranking Member Sherman for putting together this important hearing today and for our panelists for coming to share their insights and their thoughts.

While the world focuses on Islamic extremist threats that are facing countries in the Middle East and North Africa, it is critical that we not ignore this growing threat that we are seeing in other countries, in particular, in Southeast Asia which speaks to why this hearing is important.

The chairman talked about Indonesia where we saw an ISIS-linked attack in the capital of Jakarta with eight people being killed last January. Other countries in the region, also being very densely populated, where the concern is that continued attacks could lead to extensive casualties as well as great damage to those communities.

I look forward to hearing from our witnesses about what the U.S. is doing to help stop the spread of extremism in these countries. While it is not directly within this region, I do also want to mention Bangladesh, a country that continues to face growing violent jihadist problem. Last week, Nazimuddin Samad, a secular activist, was hacked to death in Dhaka following a horrific pattern that we have seen there now for the last year.

A few months ago, I introduced a resolution calling on the Government of Bangladesh to protect the rights of all of its religious minorities including Christians, Hindus, atheists, and others from these kinds of attacks. We must take action in these countries while there still is a chance to prevent groups like ISIS and their extremist ideology from growing.

Thank you very much again for being here. I look forward to hearing from you. I yield back.

Mr. SALMON. Thank you. We are joined today by Mr. W. Patrick Murphy, Deputy Assistant Secretary of State for Southeast Asia in the Department of State's Bureau of East Asia and the Pacific; Dr. Marie Richards, Deputy Counterterrorism Coordinator for Regional and Multilateral Affairs in the Department's Bureau of Counterterrorism; and Ms. Gloria Steele, Senior Deputy Assistant Administrator in the U.S. Agency for International Development's Bureau for Asia.

And we are really grateful to have all of these witnesses today, and we look forward to learning more about what is going on within the administration to deal with these issues and we will first turn to Mr. Murphy.

STATEMENT OF MR. W. PATRICK MURPHY, DEPUTY ASSISTANT SECRETARY, BUREAU OF EAST ASIA AND THE PACIFIC, U.S. DEPARTMENT OF STATE

Mr. MURPHY. Chairman Salmon, Ranking Member Gabbard, distinguished members of the subcommittee, thank you very much for the opportunity to testify today on the very important and timely issue of countering violent extremism in Southeast Asia.

I also thank the committee for its sustained support of our broad engagement across the East Asia-Pacific region exemplified by the chairman's recent travel. Thank you very much for visiting us.

The United States and our partners across Southeast Asia work together to address challenges that transcend borders, including infectious disease, trafficking in persons, wildlife, illicit narcotics, organized crime, and of course, terrorism.

As President Obama told his ASEAN counterparts at the Sunnylands Summit just this February, our global counterterrorism strategy is informed in no small part by the successes over many years of Southeast Asian nations in disrupting terrorist plots, arresting sympathizers of terrorist organizations, and establishing mechanisms to counter extremist narratives.

The January attack in Jakarta referred to by the chairman and the ranking member and other recent attacks around the world, however, demonstrate that terrorist organizations, including ISIL, can support and inspire violence almost anywhere. That is why we are building partnerships with the countries in Southeast Asia facing the most active terrorist threats including Indonesia, Malaysia, the Philippines and others as well as regional organizations like ASEAN.

Indonesia, the world's most populous Muslim majority democracy, has seen success using a rule of law based approach to counterterrorism. Government and civil society leaders have forcibly denounced ISIL. Still, according to Indonesian officials, there are about 300 Indonesians actively fighting in Iraq and in Syria. While this is a small fraction of Indonesia's 250 million plus population, the existence of such fighters and the January 14th attack in Jakarta underscore ISIL's ability to attract recruits and inspire violence in that country. In response, the Indonesian Government recently introduced legislation that would give it better tools to counterterrorism.

Indonesia is an active member of the Global Counterterrorism Forum. The country's active civil society promotes the local practice of Islam as a positive and tolerant alternative to violent extremist ideologies.

To support these efforts, we are working with Indonesia across a range of activities including training law enforcement and judicial sector officials, sharing information to prevent terrorist travel, providing technical advice on prisoner management, and supporting local counter-messaging efforts.

In Malaysia, we are also concerned about ISIL's influence, particularly through online messaging. Since 2013, Malaysian authorities have arrested over 175 terrorist suspects, primarily ISIL supporters under the country's national security legislation. Malaysia joined the Global Coalition to Counter ISIL last September and announced that it will establish a regional center to counter ISIL messaging. We support these efforts and we look forward to attending the Center's opening in the coming months.

We have also strengthened technical assistance since Malaysian Deputy Prime Minister Zahid and Secretary of State John Kerry signed a terrorist watch list sharing arrangement this past October.

In the Philippines, terrorist and criminal elements such as the Abu Sayyaf group, exploit the security environment in the Southern Mindanao region. Although some terrorist groups have pledged allegiance to ISIL, most are focused on criminality and lack strong ideological motivations. We provide, train, and equip programs to support law enforcement and military forces in the Southern Philippines which have strengthened local capabilities. We are also watching the stalled Mindanao peace process which will be important for achieving a sustainable political solution and improving the security environment for local populations.

Finally, I highlight the excellent work that ASEAN has done to strengthen collaboration in meeting these challenges, including its leading role in achieving East Asia Summit statements on ISIL in 2014 and on countering violent extremism in 2015. We are committed to working into the future with ASEAN on information sharing, border security and law enforcement cooperation.

Mr. Chairman, these partnerships demonstrate the strong and growing commitment in Southeast Asia to push back against ISIL's hateful ideology in all forms of violent extremism. With continued U.S. engagement, backed by congressional support, we are confident the countries in the region will maintain a commitment to tackling terrorism and extremism.

Thank you, and I will be happy to answer your questions.

Mr. SALMON. Thank you. Dr. Richards.

STATEMENT OF MARIE RICHARDS, PH.D., DEPUTY COUNTER-TERRORISM COORDINATOR FOR REGIONAL AND MULTILATERAL AFFAIRS, BUREAU OF COUNTERTERRORISM, U.S. DEPARTMENT OF STATE

Ms. RICHARDS. Chairman Salmon, Ranking Member Gabbard, distinguished members of the subcommittee, thank you for the opportunity to appear here today.

As you know, in the world today, we face an increasingly dynamic, diffused, and geographically decentralized set of terrorist threats. While the United States and our partners have made significant progress in reducing and denying terrorist safe havens, terrorist groups are still able to exploit local conditions and 21st century technology to attract, recruit, and conduct attacks. This is also true for Southeast Asia.

Globally, since 2012, we estimate that at least 36,000 foreign terrorist fighters from more than 120 countries have traveled to Syria and Iraq, including countries in Southeast Asia, particularly Indonesia and Malaysia. Some of these fighters have returned home, some are arrested, but as the trends continue, they are a danger to their own countries. It is clear that ISIL is inspiring terrorist activity in Southeast Asia. As the ranking member has mentioned, ISIL claimed responsibility via its English language online magazine Dabiq for the tragic attack in Jakarta this past January which was carried out by local pro-ISIS supporters.

And as the chairman has noted, our Southeast Asia partners take this threat very seriously. The law enforcement agencies have performed remarkably well in their efforts to arrest and disrupt terrorist activity. As the chairman said, the Jakarta attack could have been much deadlier if not for the effectiveness of Indonesian authorities.

That said, as President Obama has noted, we must develop more effective partnerships and tools to holistically address the evolving terrorist threat environment. We use the framework established by the U.N. Security Council Resolution 2174 which was passed in the U.N. General Assembly in 2014, sponsored by the United States. We use this as a framework for working with our partners including in Southeast Asia to put in place the fundamental reforms that will stem the flow of foreign fighters and counter violent extremism over the longer term. These points include: Increasing information sharing among countries; strengthening aviation and border security; implementing or enhancing counterterrorism legislation and supporting prosecutions and investigations; and increasing efforts to counter violent extremism particularly through strengthening community partnerships.

I will give you a few examples of how we are implementing this approach. To counter the flow of foreign terrorist fighters to conflict zones and returning from them, we are helping our partners strengthen their connectivity with Interpol. Malaysia just very recently began systematically reporting to Interpol lost and stolen travel document data. And they recently submitted 12,000 names for lost and stolen passports.

We are working with our Southeast Asia partners to build justice sector capacity. So as you know, Chairman, from your recent visit, Indonesia's improved capacity led to the conviction of Jemaah Islamiah, founder of Abu Bakar Bashir as well as the Bali bomb maker, Umar Patek, and they are both now in prison.

In the Philippines, the State Department is supporting the FBI which is assisting the Philippine Government in building terrorist financed investigations capacity. And we have had some success there as well. But even as we work to enhance security capacity, we must also work to prevent support for countering violent extremism and recruitment to violence.

So throughout Southeast Asia, we are focused on building the capacity of locally based, civil society actors in order to counteract terrorist recruitment. We are particularly looking at radicalization to violence in prisons and we are just at the beginning of this process, but we believe it is important because many people are radicalized in prison, so we are beginning to implement coming up with some pilot projects to identify terrorist prisoners, to track them through and to figure out how to remove the threat. Also, when they are brought back into the community, how do we handle that.

I will also say in closing that overall, we strongly believe that a whole of government, integrated, and coordinated approach is the only way to effectively address these threats over the longer term and our partnerships in Southeast Asia are vitally important as you have mentioned to our collective effort to counterterrorism globally as well as in the region.

I look forward to discussing these important issues with you today and thank you for holding this hearing.

[The prepared statement of Mr. Murphy and Ms. Richards follows:]

Statement of

W. Patrick Murphy
Deputy Assistant Secretary of State
Bureau of East Asian and Pacific Affairs
U.S. Department of State

Marie Richards
Deputy Coordinator
Bureau of Counterterrorism and Countering Violent Extremism
U.S. Department of State

Before the

House Foreign Affairs Committee
Subcommittee on Asia and the Pacific

April 13, 2016

Countering Extremism and the Threat of ISIS in Southeast Asia

Chairman Salmon, Ranking Member Sherman, and distinguished Members of the Subcommittee: Thank you for the opportunity to appear before you today to testify on the important and timely issue of countering violent extremism and terrorism in Southeast Asia.

We also thank the Committee for its sustained leadership in advancing U.S. interests and supporting and promoting engagement with the Asia-Pacific region. This hearing serves as an important demonstration of the expanded involvement of the United States in the region, and an important reminder that our futures are linked together.

Terrorism and Violent Extremism in Southeast Asia

The terrorist attacks last month in Brussels, in January in Jakarta, and last year in Paris, Mali, and elsewhere underscore the importance of our discussion today. We all have an enormous obligation and responsibility to find ways to defeat this scourge.

The countries in Southeast Asia that we will discuss today are committed to countering the threat of terrorism and violent extremism, in both word and action.

Governments in Southeast Asia are particularly concerned about foreign terrorist fighters (FTFs) from the region who have traveled to Syria and Iraq to fight alongside the Islamic State of Iraq and the Levant (ISIL), also known as Da'esh, and al-Nusrah Front. We estimate that by the end of 2015 approximately 1,000 Southeast Asians had traveled to the conflict zone in the Middle East. Many of these fighters may return home with battlefield experience, hardened violent ideologies, and access to global threat networks that can pose a direct threat to their home countries, as they have done in Europe. These returning foreign fighters may also enhance the capability of extremist networks within Southeast Asia, including al'Qaida affiliated groups like Jemaah Islamiya (JI). There is also the threat of "lone wolf" attacks inspired by violent extremist messaging.

We are aware of reports that ISIL is seeking to support local violent extremist groups that have declared allegiance to ISIL, and remains interested in Southeast Asia as a source of recruits and support generally. While ISIL has not formally announced the establishment of a "province" in Southeast Asia, many counterterror analysts believe they may seek to do so in the future.

The pernicious challenges of terrorism and violent extremism, however, require sustained and comprehensive efforts, including increased security cooperation and information sharing, funding, and partnerships with civil society and the private sector. Countries in Southeast Asia continue to demonstrate their commitment to countering these threats through domestic action, regionally through ASEAN, and internationally including through the Global Coalition to Counter ISIL. Partners in Southeast Asia also pledged support at the White House Summit on Countering Violent Extremism (CVE) and the Leaders' Summit on Countering ISIL and CVE at the UN General Assembly in September.

Preventing Violent Extremism from Taking Root

We must think and act broadly to prevent violent ideologies from taking hold, and to prevent terrorist networks such as ISIL from expanding their influence and linking up with regional groups, including those in Southeast Asia.

As Secretary Kerry has said, this is a fight that over the long term will require security force operations, but will also be won in schools and houses of worship; on social media; on sports fields and in workplaces; and in the homes of people across the world. We must reach those at risk before terrorist recruiters do, and amplify credible voices to counter messages of violence and hate. It requires a comprehensive approach that tackles this challenge from every angle, harnessing every tool at our disposal, and mobilizing local communities as our partners.

To help deliver on this commitment, the State Department is leading the U.S. effort abroad in coordination with the whole of our government to work with foreign governments, civil society, and individuals to prevent and counter violent extremism. Our approach is governed by five core priorities shaped at the White House Summit one year ago, and that are now part of the first-ever joint USAID and State Department strategy on preventing and countering violent extremism.

First, we are expanding partnerships to develop the expertise to better understand violent extremism and its drivers at the international, regional, national, and local levels.

Second, we are working closely with our partners—at the national and local level—in Asia and around the world to adopt more effective policies to prevent the spread of violent extremism. We are working to implement the UN Plan of Action for Preventing Violent Extremism, which asks Member States to undertake and submit national action plans to address violent extremism. In addition to the national level, we must work with sub-national actors, mayors, governors, and other municipal officials, which is why we are implementing the Strong Cities Network and other initiatives started by last year's White House CVE Summit process.

Third, we are strengthening local partnerships to address the underlying political, social, and economic factors within certain communities that may increase the likelihood that their young men and women will be targeted for recruitment by violent extremist groups. We are mobilizing public and private sector support behind these efforts through the Global Community Engagement and Resilience Fund.

Fourth, we are engaging and amplifying locally credible voices that can expose the true nature of violent extremism, its savagery, and its denial of human dignity and provide positive alternatives for opportunity, identity, trust, and resilience. Through the recently announced Global Engagement Center, we're helping to tackle terrorist messaging and recruitment efforts head on by empowering independent, positive voices from the region — voices that represent the overwhelming majority of Muslims in the world. In Southeast Asia, we are working with the Malaysian government to support the development of a regional center to counter terrorist messaging. We look forward to the launch of that center in the coming months.

Fifth, and finally, we are strengthening the capabilities of our partners to prevent radicalization in prisons and help ensure that former fighters are rehabilitated and reintegrated back into society whenever possible.

ASEAN

The United States and ASEAN have a solid record of cooperation on terrorism and countering violent extremism. ASEAN Member States share the deep U.S. concern over the threat of terrorism and the flows of Foreign Terrorist Fighters (FTFs).

In Kuala Lumpur in November, the leaders of the East Asia Summit (EAS) adopted a statement on Countering Violent Extremism that sent a clear signal of the region's determination to tackle the challenge posed by ISIL and other violent extremist groups, and to respond to their efforts to spread their ideology of violence and terrorism. This followed up on the 2014 EAS statement, where leaders committed to take actions to stem the flow of foreign fighters to and from Syria and Iraq.

The EAS is a key venue for the leaders and diplomats of this important group of nations to discuss tough issues like stopping the movement of terrorists and their money while countering their violent extremist messaging, in addition to other important security issues like the South China Sea and handling pandemic disease.

The U.S.-ASEAN Special Leaders' Summit at Sunnylands earlier this year also provided a unique opportunity for the United States to engage at the highest level on counterterrorism with all ten ASEAN nations in a free-flowing dialogue. The President and ASEAN leaders discussed how, as the ASEAN Community integrates, flows of people and goods between ASEAN Member States will also increase. As goods and people flow more freely, however, border controls and aviation security throughout ASEAN must be strengthened. The resulting

Sunnylands Declaration affirmed once more our shared resolve to lead on global challenges such as terrorism and violent extremism.

To address this issue in practical ways, at Sunnylands the President also announced a new $2 million aviation and border security program, launched at a regional workshop in Kuala Lumpur in March, which will improve ASEAN members' connectivity to global databases and real-time information sharing among countries and with INTERPOL. It will strengthen immigration security and border controls to counter the flow of FTFs. U.S. counterterrorism experts from across the U.S. government also engaged with ASEAN member countries as part of the program, including the State Department's Senior Adviser on FTFs, Ambassador Walles, and the Justice Department's representatives to INTERPOL. This project has already yielded significant results: through the assistance of INTERPOL Washington, Malaysia recently began automating daily reporting to INTERPOL of stolen and lost travel documents, becoming one of only approximately a dozen countries in the world to do so. Since going live just one month ago, Malaysia has submitted information on over 10,000 stolen and lost travel documents to INTERPOL databases.

Our increased cooperation with ASEAN on counter terrorism and CVE also offers broader benefits in the fight against trafficking in persons, drugs, wildlife, and timber; money laundering; and other transnational criminal activity.

Situations in Focus Countries

Our approach to preventing and countering terrorism and violent extremism globally and in Southeast Asia must recognize the unique situations and motivations that drive individuals to join groups like ISIL and commit acts of violence.

The countries we are focusing on today highlight the diversity in Southeast Asia, and each requires a tailored response consistent with our global approach.

Indonesia

Indonesia has seen considerable success using a civilian-led, rule-of-law-based approach in its domestic counterterrorism operations. Since the 2002 Bali bombings, Indonesia has applied sustained pressure to degrade the capabilities of terrorists and their networks operating within Indonesia's borders. Domestic terrorist groups Jemaah Islamiyah and its offshoot Jemaah Anshorut Tauhid have been degraded, though they are still active. The January 14 attack in central Jakarta, however, shows that extremists in Indonesia still have the ability to carry out small-scale attacks.

Indonesia has the world's largest Muslim population and is the world's largest Muslim-majority democracy. The vast majority of Indonesians reject ISIL and other violent extremist organizations; Indonesia's government, religious, and social leaders have repeatedly and forcefully denounced ISIL.

Indonesia recognizes the threat posed by foreign terrorist fighters and was a co-sponsor of UN Security Council Resolution (UNSCR) 2178. The United States shares Indonesia's concern that terrorist fighters returning from Iraq and Syria with new training, skills, and experience could conduct similar attacks in Indonesia. According to Indonesian officials, there are about 800 Indonesians in Iraq and Syria, although estimates fluctuate among Indonesian agencies and services. The numbers also include women, children, and non-combatants travelling out of a desire to live in the so called Islamic State. Indonesian officials claim to have identified around 300 Indonesian citizens actively involved in fighting in Iraq and Syria. They also believe that about 60 Indonesians have died in Syria and estimate that another 60 to 100 have returned to Indonesia. Most of the returnees are Indonesians and their families who were detained and deported by authorities in transit countries while en route to Syria and Iraq. Fighters may also return undetected by exploiting vulnerabilities in the land and sea borders of this vast archipelagic nation.

Abu Wardah (also known as Santoso) is the leader of Mujahidin Indonesia Timur (MIT) and is Indonesia's most-wanted terrorist. He remains at large in the remote jungle area near Poso, Central Sulawesi, where he is reported to have 20-40 followers. Santoso publicly pledged allegiance to ISIL in 2014, and in 2015 issued a message online calling for Indonesians to join ISIL in Iraq or Syria and to execute attacks on Indonesian authorities. Indonesian officials are committed to eliminating the threat posed by Santoso and MIT. A significant and sustained police operation, which includes Indonesian police's specialized counterterrorism unit Detachment 88, is ongoing. Santoso was put on Indonesia's list of domestic terrorists, under UNSCR 1373, in 2015. In March 2016, the State Department designated Santoso as a Specially Designated Global Terrorist (SDGT) under E.O. 13224.

Indonesian prosecutors actively seek to prosecute suspected terrorists – including those participating in ISIL-related activity – but current Indonesian law lacks adequate measures for criminalizing material support, traveling to join foreign terrorist organizations, or commission of extraterritorial offenses. The administration of President Joko "Jokowi" Widodo recently introduced draft legislation to give the government better legal tools to counter terrorism. It is working actively with the Indonesian legislature to secure passage of these reforms, which could happen within a few months. While new legislation is pending, prosecutors continue to use other offenses under Indonesian criminal code. Also, some of Indonesia's efforts dovetail with obligations outlined in UNSCRs 2170 and 2178. For example, Indonesia seeks to prevent the movement of terrorists, including through enhanced controls related to the issuance of identity papers. Indonesia has also implemented several of the Global Counterterrorism Forum (GCTF)'s good practices against foreign terrorist fighters.

There are roughly 200 terrorist prisoners held throughout Indonesia. Indonesian authorities are concerned they might be able to coordinate with each other, communicate with supporters outside prisons, or radicalize other, non-terrorist convicts. Prison officials are taking steps to prevent high-profile terrorist prisoners from undertaking these activities. Several terrorist convicts were paroled in 2015 after completing their prison terms, including senior leaders of Jemaah Islamiya. Indonesian officials are concerned about the potential recidivism of released terrorist prisoners. One of the attackers early this year in Jakarta had previously been convicted for terrorism-related offenses, incarcerated, and released. In addition, terrorists convicted on non-terrorism charges are not always counted or tracked through the justice system as convicted terrorists, creating a potential loophole in disengagement and de-radicalization efforts.

Indonesian officials recognize the importance of addressing radicalization to violence and CVE, though face challenges due to limited resources and the vast territory of the Indonesian archipelago. Indonesia's National Counterterrorism Agency (BNPT), which is responsible for coordinating intelligence and information among stakeholder agencies, conducts community engagement activities throughout Indonesia, often holding discussions at universities. Also, the two largest Islamic civil society organizations in the world, Nahdlatul Ulama (NU) and Muhammadiyah, are based in Indonesia and are actively involved in countering violent extremist ideologies. In addition, NU, Muhammadiya, and the Jokowi administration are promoting the Indonesian practice of Islam as a positive and tolerant alternative to violent extremist ideologies.

Our longstanding cooperation with Indonesia covers the full range of counterterrorism activities, including: training and equipment for law enforcement agencies; information-sharing both on terrorism trends and specific cases; specialized training for prosecutors and judges; technical assistance and advice on prisoner management and counter-terror finance; and support for non-governmental organizations doing grass-roots counter-messaging. In addition, our cooperation extends to international, multilateral, and regional fora. Indonesia has expanded regional and international cooperation, especially in response to the foreign terrorist fighter issue, and is an active participant in the UN, GCTF, ASEAN, APEC, and others.

The Philippines

The latest Mindanao peace process between the government and the largest Moro separatist group, the Moro Islamic Liberation Front (MILF), is currently stalled following the failure of the Philippine Congress to pass legislation needed to implement the 2014 peace deal. The continuation of this process will now be in the hands of the next administration and MILF leadership to push forward after the May 9 elections. All of the presidential candidates have indicated a willingness to continue the peace process in Mindanao although most have suggested changes to the current agreement that would require new negotiations. The resolution of the peace process with the MILF will be important for achieving a sustainable political solution to the decades long unrest in the southern Philippines, but will not prevent other armed separatist or terrorist groups from attacking government forces, private sector entities, and local rivals, even if successfully implemented.

Terrorist and criminal elements continue to exploit the poor security environment along the maritime border between the southern Philippines and eastern Malaysia, conducting kidnapping-for-ransom attacks against a range of targets, including Western tourists. Recent kidnappings include the abduction late last year of four tourists—one Norwegian national, two Canadians, and one Filipina—all of whom are still being held captive, as well as the separate kidnappings earlier this month of ten Indonesian sailors and four Malaysian sailors. The Abu Sayyaf Group, a designated foreign terrorist organization, and associated groups are believed to be behind these abductions. Despite a history of association with al-Qaida, the ASG today is mostly focused on criminality, conducting these kidnappings in the hope victims' home governments will pay ransom.

The Philippines is actively engaged in operations against high-value terrorist targets in Philippines territory. They are conducting operations routinely, and achieving some success against their targets, but also taking casualties regularly. As allies, we provide support to those efforts as requested through established train-and-equip programs provided by the Department of Defense, Department of State, and Department of Justice. At the same time, significant capability shortfalls in Intelligence, Surveillance, and Reconnaissance (ISR), transport, maritime security, and information systems remain outside the small number of high end military and police units that make sustained campaigning against the most dangerous threats difficult.

Malaysia

Malaysia is a leading member of the international community in countering ISIL, foreign terrorist fighters, and violent extremism. Malaysia joined the Global Coalition to Counter-ISIL in September 2015. Since 2013 Malaysian authorities have arrested over 175 terrorist suspects—primarily ISIL supporters—and have prosecuted approximately 40 under the country's national security legislation. Malaysia passed robust counterterrorism legislation in 2015 that criminalizes foreign terrorist travel, the receipt of terrorist training, the preparation of terrorist acts, and the possession of books and promotional materials associated with terrorist groups.

While most of those legislative changes are consistent with a rule-of-law approach to counter terrorism, we have raised our concerns that some provisions of the new laws reinstate preventive detention and could be used against political opponents of the government.

Malaysia's chairmanship of ASEAN in 2015 resulted in reaching consensus on ASEAN's statement on Countering Violent Extremism that reinforced the region's commitment to respond to violent extremist groups, including ISIL.

In September 2015, at the UN Leaders' Summit on Countering ISIL and Violent Extremism, Malaysia announced that it will establish a regional center to counter ISIL propaganda. The Department of State is supporting Malaysia's counter messaging efforts, and representatives of the Malaysian government plan to visit the United States in may for training. Senior U.S. Government officials plan to attend the center's opening in the coming months. Malaysia also recently signed two important counter terrorism and law enforcement information sharing arrangements with the United States, the Homeland Security Presidential Directive Six (HSPD-6) and Preventing and Combatting Serious Crime (PCSC). We are working closely with the Malaysian government to implement both of these arrangements promptly.

Thailand

The United States has a long history of friendship and shared interests with Thailand over the course of our 183-year-old relationship, and Thailand remains a valued law enforcement and counterterrorism partner.

Thai security officials have expressed moderate but growing concern about the potential threat to Thailand from ISIL and fighters transiting from Southeast Asia to the Middle East through

Thailand. We have no evidence of Thai citizens joining ISIL or linkages between insurgent groups in southern Thailand and ISIL, but we continue to track the situation closely.

On August 17, 2015, an explosion in central Bangkok killed 20 and injured over 120 at the Erawan Shrine, a downtown cultural destination popular with Thai and Chinese tourists. The trials of two suspects identified as Chinese Uighurs are currently underway. Some reports suggest that the attacks were related to the July 2015 forced deportation of a group of Uighur migrants to China, although Thai authorities have stated the attacks were in retaliation for a government crackdown on human trafficking networks.

Since 2004, an ethno-nationalist insurgency has claimed the lives of over 6,000 people and injured over 10,000 in Thailand's southernmost provinces. In 2015, the number of violent incidents dropped to the lowest levels in the 12-year history of the conflict although recent months have seen a troubling uptick in attacks.

The United States encourages Thailand to support an inclusive peace process that leads to a lasting resolution to the conflict. We also work with civil society groups to promote peace building and interfaith dialogue in the South. More broadly, the U.S. government funds programs to build the capacity of Thai law enforcement officials and the criminal justice system to combat terrorism and other challenges, within the legal constraints posed by the May 2014 military coup. We also support the joint U.S.-Thai International Law Enforcement Academy (ILEA) in Bangkok, which builds partner capacity and promotes cooperation especially among ASEAN Member States. We will continue to look for opportunities to expand our partnership with Thailand as we address the shared challenge of countering violent extremism in the region.

Conclusion

In conclusion, Mr. Chairman, the region encompasses a range of countries with shared and unique challenges in addressing terrorism and countering violent extremism. Regional coordination between partner countries in Southeast Asia against terror groups is improving gradually, but sustained efforts by all nations to expand cooperation among security and border and immigration services will be necessary to prevent more widespread attacks in the region.

The Department of State and USAID, working in partnership with other agencies, especially the National Counterterrorism Center, Department of Homeland Security, Department of Justice (including the FBI's Terrorist Screening Center), and the Department of Defense, have and will continue to support these countries and their people as they address the immediate security challenges and longer-term root causes of terrorism and violent extremism. With continued U.S. engagement, backed by congressional support, we are confident that the region will continue to maintain its commitment tackling this serious issue.

Thank you for the opportunity to testify today. We are pleased to answer any questions you may have.

###

Mr. SALMON. Thanks, Dr. Richards. Ms. Steele.

STATEMENT OF MS. GLORIA STEELE, SENIOR DEPUTY ASSISTANT ADMINISTRATOR, BUREAU FOR ASIA, U.S. AGENCY FOR INTERNATIONAL DEVELOPMENT

Ms. STEELE. Chairman Salmon, Ranking Member Gabbard, distinguished members of the subcommittee, thank you very much for the opportunity to testify on USAID's role in addressing the drivers of violent extremism in Southeast Asia.

Around the world, violent conflict, fragility and violent extremism pose significant threats to regional and global security. The costs of conflict in a developmental, economic and human sense are extraordinary. By neglecting the factors that drive conflict, we ignore the plight of 1½ billion people living in conflict and fragility around the world.

Knowing that violent extremists can exploit conditions of conflict and fragility, the United States Government has integrated the prevention and mitigation of conflict and the promotion of resilient, democratic societies as a key part of its defense, diplomacy and development efforts. Through this approach, and in coordination with our host countries and other donors, we help ensure progress in a broad range of priorities, including eradicating extreme poverty, while advancing the U.S.'s own security and prosperity.

At USAID, we focus on addressing the underlying socio-economic drivers of violent conflict, fragility, and violent extremism. Our multi-faceted approach considers host country commitment and capacity, builds local systems and local capacity to address the causes of violent extremism and conflict and includes women as partners in preventing conflict and building peace. Through analysis and monitoring, we ensure that our programs are effectively addressing the drivers of conflict in each unique country setting.

In the Asia-Pacific, we continue to see rapid economic growth lifting millions of people out of poverty. At the same time, growing inequality, weak governance—including corruption, social marginalization and violations of human rights are resulting in unequal access to justice and social services, particularly for members of marginalized populations. All of these issues can be drivers of instability and contribute to radicalization to violence.

USAID's work to advance democracy and promote human rights and good governance, helps to address these destabilizing factors. We encourage governments to provide all of their citizens with the space to engage in political processes, and we support civil society in voicing citizens' concerns. We work to strengthen the rule of law and government accountability in order to reduce corruption and impunity. We also build capacity for local governments to deliver health and education services. The lack of such services can create opportunities for service provision by extremist groups.

We also know that violent extremism respects no boundaries nor is it limited to any specific ideology. In countries like Burma and Sri Lanka, Muslims are also victims of violent extremism. In both countries, we are promoting tolerance and countering violence against minority, ethnic, and religious groups by encouraging the development of a balanced media and building civil society support for tolerant and inclusive speech.

Next, I will provide overviews of the three Southeast Asian countries where USAID is addressing drivers of conflict and violent extremism.

In Indonesia, impressive democratic and economic progress remains challenged by fragile institutions, corruption, and—as we saw with Jakarta's January terrorist attack—the threat of terrorism. Informed by our assessment of the drivers of violent extremism, USAID is providing access to justice and social services for the poor and most vulnerable, helping combat corruption and developing the capacity of civil society and the government to address the grievances of members of marginalized populations. We are, in addition, fostering pluralism and tolerance in Indonesia.

In the Philippines, despite significant economic and development gains, a resilient democracy and a strong civil society, the country continues to grapple with recurring insurgencies, politically motivated violence and some remaining terrorist organizations. Weak governance, including corruption, and high levels of marginalization and fragmentation have made the Autonomous Region of Muslim Mindanao particularly vulnerable.

In line with recent assessments, USAID focuses on improving local governments' ability to deliver social services in order to improve their legitimacy. We also focus on fostering greater transparency and accountability in government operations, and on fostering stronger civic engagement among local communities. We are helping 20,000 out-of-school youth to engage productively in civic and economic activities.

And finally, in southern Thailand, home to one of the most violent conflicts in the Asia-Pacific region, USAID is working to increase trust and common understanding among conflicting communities and in fostering religious tolerance.

Mr. Chairman, by addressing these destabilizing factors, our development assistance is helping to lay the foundation for security and peace for all populations in the Asia-Pacific and also the United States.

I appreciate the opportunity to testify today and look forward to your counsel and your questions. Thank you very much.

[The prepared statement of Ms. Steele follows:]

Statement of Gloria Steele
Senior Deputy Assistant Administrator, Bureau for Asia
United States Agency for International Development
Before the House Committee on Foreign Affairs, Subcommittee on Asia and the Pacific

"Countering Extremism and the Threat of ISIS in Southeast Asia"
Wednesday, April 13, 2016

Chairman Salmon, Ranking Member Sherman and Distinguished Members of the Subcommittee:

Thank you for the invitation to testify on the role of the United States Agency for International Development (USAID) in addressing the drivers of violent extremism in the Southeast Asia region. I am pleased to be testifying alongside the Deputy Assistant Secretary for the Department of State's Bureau for East Asian and Pacific Affairs, Patrick Murphy, and Deputy Coordinator Marie Richards from the Department of State's Bureau of Counterterrorism.

Violent conflict, fragility and violent extremism cross borders and present significant threats to both regional and international security. The costs of conflict — in a developmental, economic and human sense — are extraordinary. We must address the development-related factors that drive instability and the plight of the 1.5 billion people living in conflict and fragility around the world.

Knowing that violent extremists can exploit conditions of conflict and fragility, the United States Government has integrated the prevention and mitigation of conflict and the promotion of resilient, democratic societies as a key part of its defense, diplomacy and development efforts. Through this approach, and in coordination with host countries and other donors, we help to ensure progress on a broad range of priorities, including eradicating extreme poverty and advancing our own security and prosperity.

The 2015 Quadrennial Diplomacy and Development Review elevated the role of the Department of State and USAID in strengthening responsive and capable states, building secure and resilient communities and countering violent extremism. Working alongside the Department of State, USAID uses development as an effective U.S. foreign policy tool in support of the five core priorities of our joint strategy on preventing and countering violent extremism. These priorities include: 1) engaging and amplifying locally credible voices that can change the perception of violent extremism; 2) increasing support for innovative research on the drivers of violent extremism and effective interventions; 3) working closely with partners to adopt more effective policies to prevent and counter the spread of violent extremism; 4) strengthening diplomatic efforts and development approaches to address political or socioeconomic factors that can contribute to support for violent extremism and put countries and communities at high risk; and 5) strengthening the capabilities of our partners to isolate, intervene with and promote the rehabilitation and reintegration of individuals into society whenever possible.

USAID's efforts are guided by our policy on the Development Response to Violent Extremism and Insurgency, which takes an evidence-based approach to responding to the challenges associated with violent extremism, and is carefully targeted to address specific drivers and select demographic and geographic factors. This work will be coordinated by a Secretariat for

Countering Violent Extremism, which we are in the midst of establishing within USAID's Bureau for Democracy, Conflict and Humanitarian Assistance.

USAID recognizes that women are often more negatively impacted by violence, fragility and violent extremism and at the same time, often excluded from peace processes and efforts to mitigate violence and counter violent extremism. USAID seeks to empower women as equal partners in preventing conflict and building peace. We accomplish this by fostering gender equality and women's empowerment in crisis and conflict-affected countries to promote the rights and well-being of women and girls, and to foster peaceful, resilient communities that can cope with adversity and pursue development gains.

At the same time, our countering violent extremism (CVE) response cannot just be Washington driven, but must be built on local analysis and local partnerships. Rather than take a blanket approach to CVE around the world, USAID has been careful to look at how we implement CVE programs — as well as non-CVE programs that mitigate fragility and conflict — to ensure we are most effectively addressing the drivers of violent conflict, fragility and violent extremism in each unique country context. In Asia, our relevant development programming has focused on empowering communities to resist and be resilient in the face of violent extremism. While USAID has found Asian government partners' dedication to countering violent extremism and terrorism encouraging, in some countries this has also resulted in undue restrictions on civil liberties and closing space for civil society, which makes partnering with civil society and the private sector more difficult.

Addressing Destabilizing Factors in Southeast Asia

In support of the Administration's Rebalance to the Asia-Pacific, we fully recognize that our own country's future security and prosperity are inextricably tied to the Asia-Pacific region. We continue to see rapid economic growth and development lifting millions out of poverty in the region. However, we also see growing inequality and weak governance — which often result in unequal access to justice and social services, and a lack of opportunities to influence decision-making, particularly for members of minority ethnic groups and other vulnerable populations. These, along with social marginalization, violations or abuses of human rights and endemic corruption can be drivers of instability and can contribute to radicalization to violence.

USAID's development assistance in Southeast Asia addresses these destabilizing factors. We encourage governments to provide all of their citizens with the space and opportunity to engage in political processes, and we support civil society in voicing citizens' concerns. We work to strengthen the rule of law and government accountability to reduce corruption and impunity so that democratic values and processes can develop and flourish. Our assistance also improves access to — and enhances the quality of — education and health services, protects natural resources and helps to ensure that economic growth is inclusive and sustainable.

We also note that violent extremism knows no boundaries with who it impacts – victims can be of any age, gender or religion. In countries like Burma and Sri Lanka, Muslims are also victims of violent extremism. In both countries, we are promoting tolerance and countering violence against minority ethnic and religious groups by encouraging the development of a balanced media and building civil society support for tolerant and inclusive speech.

Next, allow me to provide brief overviews of countries in Southeast Asia where USAID's work to advance democracy, and promote human rights, good governance and economic growth is helping to address the risks and threats of conflict, fragility and lack of respect for human rights. Our local analyses in the region have shown that each country context and its respective drivers of conflict, fragility and violent extremism are different, so we have crafted country-specific programmatic responses to each set of problems.

Indonesia

With 240 million people, Indonesia is the world's most populous Muslim majority country and third largest democracy. It has achieved impressive progress through a remarkable democratic transformation since the late 1990s and annual economic growth of approximately 5 percent. However, its notable successes are challenged by fragile institutions, endemic corruption, and — as we saw with the January 14 terrorist attack in Jakarta — the threat of terrorism. We express our deepest condolences to the families who were affected by the terrorist attack in Jakarta, and remain a committed partner to Indonesia as the government engages in ongoing efforts to counter terrorism.

A 2013 assessment of violent extremism and insurgency in Indonesia conducted by USAID identified a number of drivers of violent extremism, as well as some key mitigating actions USAID could undertake. Informed by this assessment, USAID is promoting civic discourse on pluralism and tolerance and developing local capacity to address the grievances of members of marginalized populations. USAID also focuses on improving access to justice and service delivery to the poor and most vulnerable.

The U.S. and Indonesian governments' joint development strategy in Indonesia identifies two critical areas to address its internal development gaps, which can be drivers of violent extremism: governance, including anti-corruption efforts, and service delivery, such as education, health, water and sanitation and environmental services. USAID investments in democracy and good governance support Indonesia's stated commitment to public accountability and rule of law, broad and robust participation on the part of Indonesian civil society and the protection of the rights of all its citizens.

To strengthen government transparency, USAID has supported the country's Corruption Eradication Commission (KPK) and associated accountability institutions with targeted capacity building and technical assistance activities. These efforts have enhanced the Indonesian government's ability to address corruption and have helped improve the country's ranking on Transparency International's Corruption Perceptions Index by 30 places — moving from 118 in 2012 to 88 in 2015.

In service delivery, USAID programs support the Indonesian government in addressing the basic health, education and water and sanitation needs of its citizens across the 17,000 islands of the sprawling Indonesian archipelago. Environment sector programming also has helped to protect the country's rich natural resources and biodiversity from abuse and preserve them for the benefit of all Indonesians. In the far western province of Aceh, USAID support has improved access to justice for members of marginalized populations. New programming in the far eastern province of Papua will help to reduce gender-based violence, strengthen the performance of local government and promote respect for the rights of the Indonesian people.

Philippines
Despite significant economic growth and development gains, a resilient democracy and a strong civil society, the Philippines has a long history of recurring insurgencies, high rates of politically motivated violence, and some remaining terrorist organizations. While the current Aquino administration has made progress toward peace, the country remains exposed to threats of violent extremism and radicalization to violence.

The Autonomous Region of Muslim Mindanao (ARMM) is particularly vulnerable to drivers that favor the rise of violent extremism and influence the radicalization to violence of individuals. Recent assessments conducted jointly by USAID, the Department of State and the Department of Defense in the conflict-affected areas of ARMM identified structural "push" factors. These primarily include high levels of marginalization and fragmentation, and poor governance characterized by a preponderance of warlords and private armies, political violence, lack of transparency and accountability, corruption, poor basic service delivery and the absence of local elected officials from their constituent areas. These conditions enhance the appeal of terrorist groups, make development programs less effective and undermine the people's faith in the legitimacy of the political system.

Corrupt or abusive local governments, marginalization because of religion or ethnicity, poverty and unemployment or underemployment and the absence of basic services provide people living in the conflict-affected areas of Mindanao with deep-seated grievances. Extremist organizations, like Jemaah Islamiyah, Abu Sayyaf and Khalifa Islamiah, exploit these grievances through amplification and the offer of alternative paths that they falsely claim can only be secured through violence. Ungoverned areas, the inability to enforce the law, easy access to firearms, the presence of support bases and other risk factors provide the means to engage in violent extremist behavior.

Accordingly, USAID assistance focuses on strengthening governance in ways that promote the legitimacy and effectiveness of government and that mitigate instability and marginalization. Specifically, USAID works via a multi-pronged approach. First, we engage with local governments in conflict-prone areas to improve their delivery of basic services, and to strengthen practices that make government more transparent and accountable. Secondly, we match this work with actions in civic education, civil society strengthening and mechanisms for public participation that involve youth and adults more with their local government. Poor access to education, illiteracy, unemployment and weak representation in local and national institutions hinder youth from becoming productive members of their communities. To help address this, USAID works with more than 19,000 out-of-school youth to develop their education competencies, livelihood capabilities and life and leadership skills, so that they can engage productively in civic affairs and economic activities. USAID's economic growth, health and environment projects likewise benefit the populations of Mindanao more broadly to help overcome economic and social exclusion and strengthen resilience.

USAID is also building community capacity to prevent, mitigate and resolve conflict through a people-to-people approach that engages key peace actors who can facilitate face-to-face interactions and mobilize communities toward peace and reconciliation.

Thailand

The conflict in southern Thailand is currently one of the most violent in the Asia-Pacific region. It is concentrated along the Thailand-Malaysia border, where 94 percent of the nearly two million people identify as Muslim and 6 percent as Buddhist. This is in stark contrast to the national statistical average of 95 percent Buddhist and 5 percent Muslim. For the local population, the conflict continues to be driven by the belief that the Thai state has failed to respect their identity as Malay Muslims, and to acknowledge or effectively respond to their needs. While the conflict is often framed as a Muslim insurgency, it is mainly about Thai identity, with Islam being one important component of their identity.

Buddhism has long had a close association with the Thai state, the monarchy and national identity. Amidst tremendous social change resulting from rural to urban migration and growing income inequality, some Buddhists believe that their religion should continue to be the sole basis for social cohesion and the development of the Thai nation. A small but assertive number of Buddhist clergy are using the conflict in southern Thailand to claim that Buddhism in Thailand is under threat from within and to fuel hostility toward Islam and other religions. Nevertheless, the Thai government has resisted calls to make Buddhism the national religion, and continues to advocate for religious tolerance.

USAID is working to increase trust and common understanding among communities in the south. We focus on a people-to-people approach that incorporates cross-cultural understanding and religious tolerance. By helping to build relationships between Muslim and Buddhist communities, we are helping to change perceptions, build trust and create a social space for interaction, particularly with youth through leadership training and youth community activities. In these ways, we are helping reduce the potential for extremist violence in the south of Thailand.

Conclusion

Mr. Chairman, as you can see, the challenges facing each country are complex, which further highlights the importance of USAID's careful analysis and country-specific approach to addressing conflict and fragility in the region. By addressing these destabilizing factors in the region and tackling the drivers of violent extremism, we are laying the foundation for prosperity and stability for all populations in the Asia-Pacific. Our development assistance, along with efforts of the State Department and other U.S. Government agencies, is indispensable, and ensures that we are able to help shape a more sustainable future for the region and the world.

I appreciate the opportunity to share with you how USAID is contributing to broader U.S. Government measures to tackle the drivers of violent extremism and terrorism in Southeast Asia and look forward to hearing your counsel and questions. I welcome any questions you may have.

###

Mr. SALMON. Thank you very much. We will begin with some questions. Southeast Asian nations have very porous borders, making it difficult to track terrorists and challenging to prevent the movement of terror groups. What capabilities do the governments in Southeast Asian countries have to track foreign terrorists who are entering their borders, domestic terrorists moving within a country, and domestic terrorists going abroad for training? What is the current level of information also that is being shared between the United States and Southeast Asia nations?

Can I start with you, Mr. Murphy?

Mr. MURPHY. Thank you, Mr. Chairman. It is a great question. As you experienced in Indonesia, this is an archipelago. The same could be said for the Philippines, and parts of Malaysia. Borders throughout the region are described as porous, lacking in the infrastructure. So the key task from our perspective is information sharing, both with established international organizations among ASEAN members and across borders.

And as we heard earlier, the President announced an initiative on our part in February to increase information sharing through a $2-million program working with Interpol. And we are already seeing results, particularly in Malaysia. I can't underestimate the success of a program that automatically updates data on a daily basis to capture those last passports and identification materials.

We are also collaborating on a bilateral basis with these countries to improve information sharing and through our training programs, whether it is through my colleague's Bureau of Counterterrorism, through our anti-terrorism assistance programs, how can we improve local law enforcement capabilities, border controls, immigration standards, etcetera. And we are starting to see success. There is room for improvement and you have identified, in particular, the challenge with the geography of this region.

Mr. SALMON. Dr. Richards, did you want to comment also?

Ms. RICHARDS. Yes, thank you. Thank you for the question which is absolutely essential to what we are trying to do, particularly on stopping the flow of foreign fighters, but also in preventing safe havens that could protect all sorts of terrorists.

We have sponsored a number of regional training opportunities so that countries can come together and talk about their problems and how to work together. But I would like to highlight that we recently sent our special advisor for foreign terrorist fighters, Ambassador Jake Wallace, out to Indonesia and Malaysia to talk about the full range of improvements they might make to their own homeland security system, how we can work together, how we can implement things like this Interpol initiative. So we are working very closely with the governments, talking to them frequently to identify their gaps. This is in coordination with the DHS, Department of Homeland Security, here, and with the NCTC which, of course, looks at the threat information and can focus for where the threat is.

Mr. SALMON. That kind of segues to my next question because the United States and Australia have contributed extensive assistance to the development of Indonesia's elite counter terrorism unit, Detachment 88. How do you assess the track record of Detachment 88? And how can the United States further assist this unit? Is it

24

successful enough that we could try to duplicate it in other countries? And do you believe that Indonesia's counterterrorism efforts and particularly Detachment 88 have demonstrated sufficient regard for human rights and legal processes. Mr. Murphy?

Mr. MURPHY. Thank you, Mr. Chairman. The success of Detachment 88 is quite symbolic of the approach that Indonesia is taking to tackle the terrorism challenge. This is a civilian led, rule of law based approach. And this reflects a real transition in the way countries are tackling the challenge. And with our help and contributions, Detachment 88 is a specialized, effective, police entity to tackle counterterrorism and it has produced many arrests, successful prosecutions; I think even more importantly the thwarting of attacks and threats before they materialize. And so it is something for others to take note of and we are very pleased with the success and want to encourage more like it.

Mr. SALMON. So what can we do to maybe—maybe not exact duplicates, but similar approaches in other countries or would that be productive?

Mr. MURPHY. Well, to some degree, I think, Mr. Chairman, we are seeing similar approaches in other countries, particularly this model of emphasizing a rule of law based approach to counterterrorism, empowering civilian-led agencies to have the lead to coordinate across agencies, much like we do here in the United States. This is proving to be more effective. And Detachment 88, as I noted before having succeeded with numerous arrests, and in the case of the January attack that several of you cited, it could have been much worse. Deeply tragic, the loss of life, in particular, the four civilians, but I think many analysts see that it could have been much worse. This is the success of this rule of law based approach that Indonesia has been taking.

Mr. SALMON. Well, my time has expired. So I will turn to Representative Gabbard.

Ms. GABBARD. Thank you, Mr. Chairman. You know, we have heard numbers, estimated numbers, in particular, coming from Europe with regards to the numbers of foreign fighters who leave that region and go to places like Syria and Iraq to fight. Do you have similar estimates for Southeast Asia along those same lines?

Ms. RICHARDS. We have a few numbers in there, included in the written testimony. Essentially, we have seen about 300 foreign fighters going to Indonesia. They bring their families so the actual number is higher, and a smaller number from Malaysia, about 75. This is, of course, Indonesia is an enormous country, so per capita it is a relatively small number and much smaller than some European countries and particularly some North African countries. But one person or one small group of people can cause a lot of damage. So although the numbers are relatively small, we take them very seriously.

Ms. GABBARD. Dr. Richards, you talked about radicalization in prisons which I think is an important area that hasn't often been addressed when looking at this issue. And I wonder if you can speak in a little bit more detail about the pilot projects that you are looking at, if you have seen places where you have gotten best practices or lessons learned and I am interested to hear a little bit more about what you are looking at and what these different countries are looking at.

Ms. RICHARDS. Yes, I would be happy to. I will mention that I was in Australia last—about 6 months ago, I think, for a working group meeting of the Global Counterterrorism Forum which was mentioned here which Australia leads this working group, together with Indonesia, specifically on the question of deradicalization and reintegration. So we had representatives from a number of Southeast Asian countries. I happened to sit at a table with a Filipino prison official, but also from African countries and some other countries which face this threat. It is very dependent on the capacity of these countries, frankly.

In many of these countries, the prisons are overcrowded. There have traditionally not been ways of separating out prisoners. They don't have the capacity to provide real training, job employment prospects. They don't traditionally follow people after their release from prison and reintegrate into the society.

So the countries are working together and we are working very closely with them. We have identified best practices that would work within their societies, given their means. And this is has not being proposed as an action plan. We are doing trainings, the GCTF is doing trainings.

In addition, the United States sponsors a Department of Justice specialist, prison specialist in Indonesia, who has been working intensively with the Indonesian prison officials, as I said, starting with a fairly small population, but to provide a model for how we can—they can identify these prisoners and gradually, ideally deradicalize them, but at least keep them from radicalizing within the prison community.

Ms. GABBARD. You mentioned some of the lack of resources in tracking or following people when they leave. With the relatively small number of foreign fighters who leave and then come back to whether it is Indonesia or Malaysia, are they—do they have the resources and are they tracking and identifying who these individuals are?

Ms. RICHARDS. In the case of foreign fighters, I am not sure there is a problem. In the case of Malaysia, for example, they have arrested all the foreign fighters they have identified who came back. It is eight of them. And they are all in prison.

We are more concerned about some of the terrorists who have been in prison for a while, particularly the Bali bomber terrorists who are due to be released. In fact, their on-going release is now. So we, as the United States, and also the Indonesian Government, the Australian Government, throughout the region, they are very concerned about what these people could do when they are on the outside.

Ms. GABBARD. You mentioned the 300 though from Indonesia, for example.

Ms. RICHARDS. Yes, the 300 went. Sixty have been stopped. They have been stopped through this kind of information sharing. Obviously, these are rough numbers and there may be some out there that we are not aware of. But the problem is more a long-term problem that we see as with many of these issues.

Ms. GABBARD. Thank you. And Mr. Murphy, I think you spoke about the online messaging issue and a counter online messaging initiative that is being implemented. Can you speak about this and how they have seen where it has worked and what they are modeling this after?

Mr. MURPHY. Yes, thank you, Congresswoman. Online messaging is one of those tools that ISIL has used to some effect in Southeast Asia with its messages of falsehoods, of mischaracterizing Islam and supposed threats against Islam.

Ms. GABBARD. This is something that we see here, as well.

Mr. MURPHY. That is correct. It is a global challenge. So Southeast Asia is not immune from it. The countries that we partner with in this region understand that very, very well. Malaysia, with its stepped-up cooperation with the international community initiated on its own a messaging center that will have regional reach. They plan to stand that up in the coming months in Kuala Lumpur and we look forward to being there, being there and supporting this process. It takes a lot of work to counter the messaging and it has to be from our perspective a local effort. That can't be done from the United States or elsewhere. We have good partners, not just in government, but in civil society. I will give you an example, Congresswoman. In Indonesia, two of the largest Islamic civil society organizations in the world are located there and are some of the most vocal voices when it comes to condemning ISIL and the message of hatred. Those are the kind of partners we are looking at empowering, working with to help with this counter messaging kind of effort.

Ms. GABBARD. Yes, Dr. Richards.

Ms. RICHARDS. Congresswoman, I just want to take a very short moment to address your comment on Bangladesh because we completely agree with you. The State Department will be sending a high-level team out to Bangladesh next month to consult with them on what their problem is and how we can help them and we are doing quite a lot in Bangladesh. We can discuss separately.

Ms. GABBARD. Thank you. I appreciate you mentioning that. Thanks.

Mr. SALMON. Thank you. Mr. Rohrabacher.

Mr. ROHRABACHER. Thank you very much, Mr. Chairman. And I appreciate you taking the time and effort to make sure that this hearing happened today on a very significant issue. I remember that back in 2001, the first real attack that I heard of after 9/11 happened in Bali where—and I happen to represent Surf City USA, Huntington Beach, and we took that very seriously, where just a group of surfers who were frankly enjoying themselves in the evening at one of their local bars, it was blown up and these are people who were no threat to anyone which indicated that we were, the world, when you combine that with what happened on 9/11, that the world was into a new challenge that we have faced and the good people of the world.

I will have to say that there is some skepticism on the part of some of us as to the way the administration is handling this unique challenge that we face. And I will say there are hints of that today, although let me just say that I have no doubt that each one of you are doing the very best job you can and I am grateful for it. I have three children who I want to live in a safer world. But I think that quite often this administration is mistaking the fight against radical Islamic terrorists, by the way a phrase which I have to note doesn't seem to be able to be spoken not only by our President, but even by the witnesses who come to Congress. I never heard that radical Islamic terrorism or just even Islamic terrorism. Instead, I hear about violent extremists as if we are not talking about Islamic terrorists at all. We are talking about extremists, whoever they are. No, what has happened is radical Islamic terrorists have declared war on the United States and on Western civilization, meaning our allies in this world. And I am sorry that you can't use those words because it takes away from the confidence that we could have in your efforts.

And in the fact that that seems to be something that indicates something, that it would be in my mind that you are taking a law-enforcement approach versus a counterterrorism approach. And law enforcement is a great deal different than counterterrorism. Law enforcement is that you basically will try to find out who has committed a crime and punish them for it and maybe to go out and to find out who is in a gang and try to get a message as you have described, and messages from people in Indonesia who are speaking out, Muslims are speaking out against this terrorism. But counterterrorism is you are dealing with monsters who kill innocent women and children, target them in order to terrorize a population. It is different than law enforcement. Totally different—not totally, but major differences in those approaches.

Let me ask you specifically, and again, I am afraid this administration and what I have heard today does not sway me from my apprehension that there is a problem there in the definition of what we are trying to do and the definition of who we are trying to get to or who we are trying to eliminate. Because we are not trying to eliminate violent extremists. That is not what is attacking our families and people throughout the world. It is radical Islamic terrorists.

Let me ask you about the Philippines, which I have spent a great deal of time in over the years. I understand there was recently an Abu Sayyaf terrorist attack in the Philippines. Is that correct? Can you give me some details on that?

Mr. MURPHY. Thank you, Congressman. Indeed, a subunit, a splinter group of the ASG was involved in a conflict with Filipino security forces over the weekend. We understand this cost the lives of several dozen Filipino security force members and we express our deepest condolences. This kind of violence, kind of conflict, costs real in terms of human lives and local security.

However, it does not diminish the fact that the Philippines has had success in recent years in degrading the capabilities of this particular group. Small numbers are left. They are a threat. The Philippines is taking it very seriously, but achieving success.

Mr. ROHRABACHER. Yes, we had a special forces team there for a number of years and they did a great job. And let me also note the State Department is focused on that part of the Philippines and has done a good job as well. And we should remember that Ramzi Yousef, after planning the first terrorist attack on the World Trade Center, where he ended up. He ended up in the Philippines and he was there—I am still trying to find evidence that was in some way associated with the Abu Sayyaf terrorist network and other people who are affiliated with that.

This is a major threat in the world today. This region is not immune. It could get a lot worse. I have reports that the situation in Mindanao is a lot worse than those of us who have been watching and believed it to be. So I look forward to working with you, as well as with our chairman, to make sure we all do our best to defeat the radical Islamic terrorists who want to murder us. Thank you very much, Mr. Chairman.

Mr. SALMON. If you don't mind, I would like to ask one more question. I mentioned that when I was over there I visited one of the madrasas. I think when a lot of my constituents hear the term madrasa, they conjure up something in their mind because some of these madrasas in the Middle East have been used for recruiting purposes and indoctrinating purposes. But I learned while I was there that the term madrasa just means boarding school. That is the term that they use and it is a very typical way of educating the children.

You mentioned, Mr. Murphy, that you are very concerned about the radicalization, the recruiting that happens in prison. Are you concerned about that possibly happening in some of the schools? And how well do you think these governments are doing at dealing with those threats as well?

Mr. MURPHY. Mr. Chairman, I will again thank you for leading a delegation out to Indonesia and would encourage all members of the committee to visit Southeast Asia. Our embassies and consulates will take good care of you and you can see first hand our engagement across the board in Southeast Asia which is really——

Mr. SALMON. If I could just say, the folks in our embassy there were second to none. They were amazing, really, really talented, wonderful individuals and I couldn't be prouder. But every time I go across the world and I visit an embassy, I always feel the same. I think that they are the brightest and the best that we have to offer in our society and I really appreciate the great work that they do.

Mr. MURPHY. Thank you, Mr. Chairman. I will carry that message directly to Jakarta in a week and a half when I will be with our Ambassador Blake and his team. Thank you very much for that.

You know, you have identified one of the issues that we watch very closely and that is what are the vulnerabilities to extremism? And what are the drivers? And there are a whole host and my colleagues can speak to that as well in terms of social inequities, economic opportunities. For some, it might be religious related. I think the important thing to look at from the U.S. perspective is our whole of government broad approach to Southeast Asia, our rebalance to Asia under this administration, but our engagement in so many different areas. Youth is one of them, youth and education. We have a young, Southeast Asia leadership initiative, YSEALI, that has been enormously successful in drawing over 50,000 Southeast Asian youth to partner with our missions, with our President, to engage in a whole host of opportunities, innovation, technology, education exchanges. These are the future leaders of the region and the youth hold a lot of promise.

I don't think we see any particular vulnerabilities in religious faith-based schools and education institutions, but we do see a very broad need for local governments, local entities to message very carefully to counter the false messaging that is coming from ISIL. And schools and youth would be no exception.

Mr. SALMON. Thank you. Representative Gabbard, did you have another question? No. Well, thank you very, very much. This has been very, very helpful. We appreciate you coming and sharing what the administration is doing in Southeast Asia about global terrorism. So thank you very much. We appreciate it and without further ado, this meeting is adjourned.

[Whereupon, at 3:08 p.m., the subcommittee was adjourned.]

APPENDIX

MATERIAL SUBMITTED FOR THE RECORD

SUBCOMMITTEE HEARING NOTICE
COMMITTEE ON FOREIGN AFFAIRS
U.S. HOUSE OF REPRESENTATIVES
WASHINGTON, DC 20515-6128

Subcommittee on Asia and the Pacific
Matt Salmon (R-AZ), Chairman

April 6, 2016

TO: MEMBERS OF THE COMMITTEE ON FOREIGN AFFAIRS

You are respectfully requested to attend an OPEN hearing of the Committee on Foreign Affairs, to be held by the Subcommittee on Asia and the Pacific in Room 2172 of the Rayburn House Office Building (and available live on the Committee website at http://www.ForeignAffairs.house.gov):

DATE: Wednesday, April 13, 2016

TIME: 2:00 p.m.

SUBJECT: Countering Extremism and the Threat of ISIS in Southeast Asia

WITNESSES: Mr. W. Patrick Murphy
Deputy Assistant Secretary
Bureau of East Asia and the Pacific
U.S. Department of State

Marie Richards, Ph.D.
Deputy Counterterrorism Coordinator for Regional and Multilateral Affairs
Bureau of Counterterrorism
U.S. Department of State

Ms. Gloria Steele
Senior Deputy Assistant Administrator
Bureau for Asia
U.S. Agency for International Development

By Direction of the Chairman

The Committee on Foreign Affairs seeks to make its facilities accessible to persons with disabilities. If you are in need of special accommodations, please call 202/225-5021 at least four business days in advance of the event, whenever practicable. Questions with regard to special accommodations in general (including availability of Committee materials in alternative formats and assistive listening devices) may be directed to the Committee.

COMMITTEE ON FOREIGN AFFAIRS

MINUTES OF SUBCOMMITTEE ON _____*Asia and the Pacific*_____ HEARING

Day___*Wednesday*___Date_____*4/13/16*_____Room_____*2172*_____

Starting Time ____*2:21pm*____ Ending Time ____*3:08pm*____

Recesses |___| (____to ____) (____to ____) (____to ____) (____to ____) (____to ____) (____to ____)

Presiding Member(s)

Salmon

Check all of the following that apply:

Open Session ☑
Executive (closed) Session ☐
Televised ☐

Electronically Recorded (taped) ☐
Stenographic Record ☐

TITLE OF HEARING:

Countering Extremism and the Threat of ISIS in Southeast Asia

SUBCOMMITTEE MEMBERS PRESENT:

DesJarlais, Perry, Chabot, Duncan, Rohrabacher, Brooks
Gabbard, Meng

NON-SUBCOMMITTEE MEMBERS PRESENT: *(Mark with an * if they are not members of full committee.)*

HEARING WITNESSES: Same as meeting notice attached? Yes ☑ No ☐
(If "no", please list below and include title, agency, department, or organization.)

STATEMENTS FOR THE RECORD: *(List any statements submitted for the record.)*

TIME SCHEDULED TO RECONVENE_____
or
TIME ADJOURNED ____*3:08*____

Subcommittee Staff Director

Question for the Record submitted to
Deputy Coordinator Marie Richards
By Representative Matt Salmon (#1)
Subcommittee on Asia and the Pacific
House Foreign Affairs Committee
April 13, 2016

Question:

Southeast Asian nations face terrorist threats on multiple levels, including fighters returning from conflict zones, the strengthening of regional terrorist groups, and the radicalization of individuals. Which source of radicalism and recruitment worries you the most and why? Are there particular sources of radicalism – such as recruitment in prisons or madrassas – that the United States should devote increased attention to?

Answer:

Countries across Southeast Asia are actively working to address terrorist threats and degrade the ability of terrorist groups to operate in the region. While sites or sources of radicalization to violence are varied, prisons are often the most prolific. Inmates may feel resentment towards the system; becoming a part of a group within a prison enhances one's personal security as well as sense of belonging; and violent extremists can utilize prison networks to help facilitate attacks on civilian targets, as was the case prior to the January 2016 attacks in Indonesia.

Individuals can also be radicalized to violence through intolerance or radical teachings at Madrassas. However, Muslim academic communities in Southeast Asia are strong advocates for promoting moderate Islam both at home and abroad, and many governments in Southeast Asia have established numerous regulatory mechanisms for monitoring the educational standards and ideology taught at religious schools. The spread of radicalism in cyberspace is also a concern.

In partnership with governments, the Department of State works to strengthen legal counterterrorism frameworks for both online and offline threats, improve prison institutions, build partner capacity to investigate and prosecute terrorism cases, increase regional cooperation and information sharing, and address critical border and aviation security gaps, while respecting human rights and fundamental freedoms such as freedom of expression and freedom of religion. We also prevent and counter violent extremism in partnership with civil society and host governments by addressing specific societal dynamics and drivers of radicalization to violence to counter the ideology, messaging, and recruitment methods that violent extremist groups employ to attract new recruits and foment violence, including online. We recognize that our efforts are most effective in local languages, and are working toward tailored approaches for each country's needs. We will continue to devote resources to areas where there is mutual interest and sustainable results.

Question for the Record Submitted to
Deputy Assistant Secretary W. Patrick Murphy
Representative Matt Salmon (#2)

Question:

Regarding madrassas, Deputy Assistant Secretary Murphy said during the hearing that the administration doesn't "see any particular vulnerabilities in religious faith-based schools," while acknowledging that youth are at risk from extremist influences. Do religious institutions funded from outside the region present or contribute to extremist or radical influences within Southeast Asia?

Answer:

Muslim academic communities in Southeast Asia generally are strong advocates for promoting moderate Islam, both at home and abroad. Governments in the region have established numerous regulatory mechanisms for monitoring the educational standards and ideologies of religious schools.

In some cases, foreign-funded private institutions are not subject to these national educational regulations. Governments recognize the implications of unregulated education and take steps to monitor the potential spread of violent extremist ideologies through educational institutions.

We work with Muslim academic communities to counter violence extremist messages. Our CVE programs empower civil society, including religious leaders and students, to speak out against violence and promote tolerance, diversity, and moderation.

Question for the Record Submitted to
Deputy Assistant Secretary W. Patrick Murphy
Representative Matt Salmon (#3)

Question:

The Islamic State has proven adept at radicalizing young Muslims from moderate and educated backgrounds, and Southeast Asia has a surfeit of young people who fit this description. How does the FY2017 budget request reflect steps taken to protect young Muslims in Southeast Asia from radicalizing messaging? What is the U.S. strategy to protect young people in the region from radicalizing influences? Is YSEALI the primary pillar of such a strategy? If so, please explain why this innovation and entrepreneurship program is the best counterterror messaging tactic in the U.S. toolkit.

Answer:

The FY2017 budget request includes a range of efforts to protect young people from radicalizing influences through direct Public Diplomacy programming as well as Counterterrorism, USAID, and Global Engagement Center funding requests. These programs help to improve education, bolster youth employment, defend human rights, support the rule of law, empower underserved populations, enhance regional connectivity, and promote civic engagement.

Various public diplomacy programs support these efforts, including English-language training, academic and professional exchanges, regional youth programs, alumni grants programs, and many sports and cultural programs. Our diplomatic missions engage local populations through speakers programs, American Corner activities, Information Resource Centers, Officer site visits, and digital video conferencing.

While YSEALI is our principal youth engagement program for Southeast Asia, its themes do not specifically cover CVE and the issue does not equally affect all 10 countries that participate in YSEALI. It is therefore only part of our strategy to combat radicalizing influences in EAP. The program empowers youth – including young, educated Muslims – to address issues such as youth employment, education, human rights, and civic engagement constructively. Giving youth the tools to be effective change agents within the rule of law deters them from choosing violence or extremism as the means to achieve social change. Additionally, YSEALI builds an affinity for the United States as the partner who will help them achieve personal, local and regional success.

Question for the Record Submitted to
Senior Deputy Assistant Administrator Gloria Steele
Representative Matt Salmon (#4)

Question:

The U.S. Joint Special Operations Task Force–Philippines (JSOTF-P) assisted the Philippine armed forces and gained the upper hand against the terrorist Abu Sayyaf Group in the southern Philippines, before beginning to withdraw in 2014. Our development efforts in the southern Philippines were also closely coordinated with our counterterrorism efforts. How would you describe the overall effectiveness of US counterterrorism assistance?

Answer:

Militarily, U.S. counterterrorism assistance in the Philippines has worked very well since the start of JSOTF-P in 2002. The United States deployed footprint was relatively small. The task force focused on supporting the host nation's military and over time helped to degrade several Department of State designated terror groups to the point where they no longer pose credible threats to areas outside of their area of operations. With the assistance of JSOTF-P, the

Armed Forces of the Philippines grew more and more capable. Since the withdrawal of JSOTF-P, the AFP has been steadily carrying out counterterror operations against high value targets with success. Some observers credit JSOTF-P with forcing the Moro Islamic Liberation Front (MILF) to the negotiating table.

As noted, development efforts in the Southern Philippines were coordinated with the efforts of the Philippine military. As outlined in an assessment by the RAND Corporation, this mutually beneficial partnership allowed the U.S. Agency for International Development (USAID) and JSOTF-P to exchange staff in order to increase collaboration and effectiveness, and reduce redundancy within their offices. Additionally, JSOTF-P played an integral role in ensuring the safety of USAID staff by providing a secure location in Mindanao, helping USAID monitor and evaluate projects in more-remote and dangerous areas, and providing safe transport of USAID staff via JSOTF-P air and maritime assets. This partnership enabled increased success within efforts on both fronts, and ensured that USAID could continue its development programming in Mindanao – focused on social service provision strengthening, fostering transparency and accountability within the government and stronger civic engagement among local communities, and assisting out-of-school youth to engage productively in civic and economic activities. Politically, however, the southern Philippines is a good case study of the limits of U.S. assistance. The judicial process is still slow. Corruption is still an issue. The terrorist groups that operate in the area can still recruit, rearm, and reemerge if a last peace is not anchored by a political solution to the conflict. Many of the societal issues are still being worked on by our Philippine partners and we are also working to provide development assistance to the southern Philippines to address these issues.

Question for the Record Submitted to
Senior Deputy Assistant Administrator Gloria Steele
Representative Matt Salmon (#5)

Question:

In designing anti-poverty or education programs in Southeast Asia, how much do counter-terrorism and de-radicalization goals factor into the program-design process? For instance—when working in conflict areas in the southern Philippines, how do you design capacity-building programs that have the greatest impact in countering militant narratives? How do you choose and assess local partners for such projects?

Answer:

The U.S. Agency for International Development (USAID) takes a strategic approach to responding to the challenges associated with violent extremism by carefully targeting our efforts to address specific drivers and select demographic and geographic factors. In our response to countering violent extremism globally, we build our approach on local analysis and local partnerships and carefully examine how we implement programs to ensure that we are most effectively addressing the drivers of violent conflict, fragility and violent extremism in each unique country context.

In Southeast Asia, our relevant development programming has focused on empowering communities to resist and be resilient in the face of violent extremism. With the exception of the programs in the southern Philippines, we have not designed anti-poverty or education programs in the region with the explicit goal of counter-terrorism and de-radicalization. Rather, we have analyzed the drivers of violent extremism in various individual countries and based our programmatic response on how best USAID could address them.

In Indonesia, for example, USAID found through our analyses that we were best poised to address drivers of violent extremism through the promotion of civic discourse on pluralism and tolerance and the development of local capacity to address the grievances of members of marginalized populations. We have also found success in improving access to justice, strengthening government transparency, and improving service delivery to the poor and most vulnerable.

In the southern Philippines, where USAID does have dedicated anti-poverty and education programs in Mindanao, we are working with more than 19,000 out-of-school youth to develop their education competencies, livelihood capabilities and life and leadership skills, so that they can engage productively in civic affairs and economic activities. USAID's economic growth, health and environment projects likewise benefit the populations of Mindanao more broadly to help overcome economic and social exclusion, and strengthen resilience. More broadly, USAID also engages with local governments in conflict-prone areas to improve service delivery and strengthen government transparency and accountability, as well as engaging in civic education and civil society development.

Question for the Record Submitted to
Deputy Assistant Secretary W. Patrick Murphy
Representative Matt Salmon (#6)

Question:

The United States is pursuing a variety of efforts to enhance cooperation and build capacity with nations in the region. Broadly, how does U.S. policy address the underlying causes for the spread of radical Islam (rather than the symptoms only)? What are these causes, especially in relation to Southeast Asia? Please give specific examples of USAID's work in the region that has addressed root causes of militancy. Have such programs been effective?

Answer:

Countering violent extremism (CVE) refers to proactive actions to counter efforts by violent extremists to radicalize, recruit, and mobilize followers to violence and to address specific factors that facilitate violent extremist recruitment and radicalization.

This includes building specific alternatives, capabilities, and resiliencies in targeted communities, populations, and government institutions to reduce the risk of radicalization and recruitment to violence.

To be effective, CVE efforts must be guided by ongoing research and analysis of the local context of, factors associated with, and most effective interventions in preventing and countering radicalization and recruitment to violence. The Department's Bureau of Conflict and Stabilization Operations (CSO) is focused on these key issues as part of its support to Department-wide CVE efforts. Department-wide CVE efforts also benefit from research collaboration with USAID.

To date, USAID has conducted studies on the drivers of violent extremism in Bangladesh, Central Asia, Indonesia, Malaysia, the Philippines, and Thailand. Based on the findings of those studies, USAID has determined it is best positioned in Southeast Asia to support efforts to address the drivers of violent extremism through development programming that tackles growing inequality, weak governance – including corruption, social marginalization, and violations of human rights that are resulting in unequal access to justice and social services, particularly for members of marginalized populations. All of these issues can be drivers of instability and can contribute to radicalization to violence.

For example, in the Philippines, USAID 's Governance, Accountability, and Engagement (ENGAGE) project aims to promote good governance and accountability in the six conflict areas of Mindanao including Cotabato City, Marawi City, Zamboanga City, Isabela City, Southern Basilan, and Jolo. The project helps to strengthen the capacity, legitimacy, transparency, and accountability of local government and increases citizen involvement in governance through civic education, civil society strengthening, and by promoting participatory mechanisms. Promoting the legitimacy and effectiveness of the government helps mitigate instability and marginalization within local communities.

Question for the Record Submitted to
Deputy Assistant Secretary W. Patrick Murphy
Representative Matt Salmon (#7)

Question:

The United States coordinates, participates in, and advises a number of global and regional counterterrorism-related policymaking or information exchange bodies in which Asian governments participate. How do you assess the level of counterterrorism cooperation between Southeast Asian governments and the United States?

Answer:

Cooperation with Southeast Asian nations is strong and growing. The discussion on counterterrorism at the ASEAN Sunnylands Summit in February demonstrated our robust partnership and the political will of countries to tackle terrorism issues. Southeast Asian nations have also been strong supporters of the Global Coalition to Counter ISIL and the White

House Summit on Countering Violent Extremism. Across Southeast Asia, we are working with partners at the national and local level on a full range of counterterrorism programs to strengthen information sharing and border security, enhance justice sector and law enforcement capacity, strengthen prisoner rehabilitation and reintegration, and counter violent extremist recruitment and messaging.

Question for the Record Submitted to
Senior Deputy Assistant Administrator Gloria Steele
Representative Matt Salmon (#8)

Question:

Some observers call for an increase in civil society activism to educate and inspire communities to stem the tide of terrorist activity. What role do you see for Southeast Asian civil society groups to play in countering militancy in the region? How has USAID assisted Southeast Asian civil society groups to do such work, and what other opportunities do you see for the United States to further these efforts?

Answer:

The participation of civil society in countering militancy in the region is essential. Civil society's ability to promote pluralism and tolerance within their communities, and their role in engaging with and empowering often marginalized parts of society – such as vulnerable communities, women, and youth – is a key in addressing the drivers of instability and violent extremism in any region.

In Southeast Asia, USAID is working with civil society organizations across the region to empower and support them as they continue to voice citizens' concerns and promote tolerant and inclusive speech between different groups. For example, in Indonesia, we are investing in democracy and good governance to increase broad and robust participation on the part of Indonesian civil society in the continued development of their country. Similarly, in the Philippines, USAID is supporting civic education, civil society strengthening, and mechanisms for public participation of youth in their local government. By supporting civil society participation in both countries, we are enabling them to voice the interests of marginalized populations to their government and hopefully therefore increase government responsiveness. These efforts help to strengthen government legitimacy and effectiveness, and can lead to the mitigation of instability and marginalization.

However, in some countries in Asia, we have seen that government efforts to counter violent extremism and terrorism has resulted in undue restrictions on civil liberties and a closing space for civil society, thus making partnering with civil society more difficult. The U.S. government will continue to support civil society and voice concern to country governments regarding their closing space, and our development assistance will continue to strengthen their capacity so that they can help address the drivers of violent extremism and instability within their own communities.

Question for the Record submitted to
Deputy Coordinator Marie Richards
By the Subcommittee on Asia and the Pacific (#9)

Question:

In January 2016, terrorists carried out a deadly attack in the capital of Indonesia, including bombing a mall and police post. Did the January 2016 Jakarta attack potentially mark a return by militants in Southeast Asia to a focus on Western targets in the region? Are Paris-style attacks with small arms more likely than bombings in the region?

Answer:

Indonesian government officials have said that local militants from the pro-ISIL organization, Jemaah Anshourt Daulah (JAD) were responsible for the attack. Indonesian police killed all four attackers and claim to have arrested all those based in Indonesia that were involved in planning or executing the attack. Indonesian police continue to investigate, detect, and disrupt emerging terrorist threats and plots, and an effective and sustained counterterrorism campaign led by the Indonesian National Police since 2002 has substantially degraded the operational capacity of terrorist organizations operating in Indonesia. The January 2016 attack illustrated that extremists in Indonesia still have both the willingness and the capability to carry out small-scale violent attacks, but the attacks also demonstrated the effectiveness of Indonesian law enforcement in containing and neutralizing such threats. As threats change – for example, the rising threat of foreign fighters – we adapt our cooperation to meet them, and we continually discuss new avenues of cooperation.

Question for the Record Submitted to
Deputy Assistant Secretary W. Patrick Murphy
Representative Matt Salmon (#10)

Question:

Some argue that Indonesia has reached a dangerous point in which various disparate groups may seek to conduct attacks more lethal than the January attacks in Jakarta, in a misguided effort to prove legitimacy and recruit more members. Do you agree with this assessment? If so, what can the United States do to help Indonesia prevent such catastrophes from occurring?

Answer:

The Indonesian National Police have substantially degraded the operational capacity of terrorist organizations operating in Indonesia since 2002, but the January 14, 2016, attack in Jakarta illustrated that violent extremists in Indonesia still have both the willingness and the capability to carry out small-scale violent attacks.

As threats have changed – for example, the rising threat of foreign fighters – we have adapted our cooperation to meet them and are always discussing new avenues of cooperation. We have worked closely with Indonesia for a number of years on counterterrorism capacity-building, including: training and equipment for law enforcement agencies; information-sharing; specialized training for prosecutors and judges; and technical assistance and advice on prisoner management and counter-terror finance.

In addition, USAID is addressing the drivers of instability in Indonesia by fostering pluralism and tolerance. USAID assistance is increasing access to justice and social services for the poor and most vulnerable, helping to combat corruption, and developing the capacity of civil society and the government to address the grievances of members of marginalized populations.

Question for the Record submitted to
Deputy Coordinator Marie Richards
By the Subcommittee on Asia and the Pacific (#11)

Question:

Do Southeast Asian governments have legal regimes strong enough to monitor and address terrorist threats? Please discuss Malaysia's 2015 Prevention of Terrorism Act, and Indonesia's current efforts to amend and strengthen its 2003 Anti-Terrorism Law. Do you feel both countries are striking a proper balance in giving their police greater capacity to fight terrorism, and protecting human rights and freedom of expression?

Answer:

It is important for countries to ensure that their laws adequately address the complex and evolving nature of the global terrorist threat, including appropriate provisions to counter foreign terrorist fighters. The text of proposed legislative reforms to Indonesian's counterterrorism laws is still being deliberated within the Indonesian legislature. Indonesian lawmakers, government officials, and civil society leaders are engaged in an open, active, and appropriate debate regarding the contents of the draft amendment. We believe it is possible to actively counter terrorism while also protecting human rights.

In 2012 Malaysia abolished its decades old Internal Security Act, which had been used to detain without trial individuals deemed a threat to national security, including suspected violent extremists. With the passage of the Security Offenses (Special Measures) Act (SOSMA) in 2012, Malaysia began transitioning to a rule-of-law based approach to counterterrorism. Under SOSMA and related counterterrorism legislation passed in 2015, Malaysia has successfully prosecuted through its courts approximately 40 ISIL sympathizers and other terrorist supporters.

The United States has expressed concerns about certain provisions of the 2015 Prevention of Terrorism Act (POTA) that provide for detention without trial or other limitations on an individual's freedom of movement. In both private conversations and public statements, senior

U.S. officials have emphasized to Malaysian government interlocutors the importance of maintaining human rights standards and due process in countering terrorism. We have also raised concerns about the selective use of the Sedition Act and other laws to stifle dissent and political opposition at the highest levels.

Question for the Record Submitted to
Deputy Assistant Secretary W. Patrick Murphy
Representative Matt Salmon (#12)

Question:

In recent years, Malaysia has made progress toward eligibility for the U.S. Visa Waiver Program (VWP), which would allow Malaysian citizens to travel to the United States for up to 90 days without a visa. Are Malaysia's domestic counter-terrorism measures sufficient to allow Malaysia to proceed with its application for the VWP? Or does the United States need to see evidence of significant improvement before moving forward with Malaysia's participation in the VWP?

Answer:

The Department of State and Department Homeland Security have been working with Malaysia to meet the statutory requirements for Visa Waiver Program eligibility. The statutory requirements – including information sharing agreements and the regular reporting of lost travel documents – are important to our counterterrorism efforts, and Malaysia has made great progress on these fronts. DHS manages the VWP program in coordination with State, so State defers to that agency any questions about Malaysia's participation in the program.

Question for the Record Submitted to
Deputy Assistant Secretary W. Patrick Murphy
Representative Matt Salmon (#13)

Question:

The Government of the Philippines and the Moro Islamic Liberation Front spent a long time negotiating the Comprehensive Agreement on the Bangsamoro (CAB), which would provide greater political and economic autonomy to the Moro people and could potentially bring peace to the southern region of the Philippines. If the agreement is not passed by the Philippine Congress soon, what would be its impact be on radicalization in Mindanao and Sulu? Would it lead to feelings of political disenfranchisement and lesser economic opportunity among Muslim communities? Would its impact reduce the attractiveness of extremist groups, including Moro Islamic Liberation Front (MILF) splinter groups, and activities?

Answer:

The MILF appears content to wait until the May 9 election results are determined before making any decisions. We cannot rule out the possibility that the MILF will return to fighting, however, if the next administration does not pursue or secure a peace agreement that is satisfactory to the organization. Such an action will obviously have a very negative impact on the Mindanao region since open source reporting estimates the MILF strength to be approximately 10,000-12,000 armed fighters.

Even if the MILF accepts a peace agreement suggested by the new administration, hardline members may still balk at the agreement and form splinter groups, increasing the likelihood for violence in the region.

Nevertheless, political disenfranchisement and lesser economic opportunity can be a factor that leads some to violent extremism. USAID is supporting civic education, civil society strengthening, and mechanisms for public participation of youth in their local government. These efforts help to strengthen government legitimacy and effectiveness, and can lead to the mitigation of instability and marginalization.

**Question for the Record Submitted to
Deputy Assistant Secretary W. Patrick Murphy
Representative Matt Salmon (#14)**

Question:

Certain domestically oriented terrorist groups maintain connections with other terrorist groups in the region; this is especially prevalent where the borders of Indonesia, Malaysia, and the Philippines converge. What joint capabilities do Indonesia, Malaysia, and the Philippines have to combat terrorism moving among their borders? What is the United States doing to encourage regional cooperation?

Answer:

ASEAN has led the effort to increase cooperation among member states, including Indonesia, Philippines, and Malaysia. ASEAN recognizes that improved law enforcement capacity, information sharing, and cooperative habits are essential elements of counterterrorism. ASEAN led the adoption of a statement on cooperation against foreign terrorist fighters at the 2014 East Asia Summit (EAS), and a statement on countering violent extremism at EAS in 2015. In addition, the United States is working with ASEAN to build the capacity of its Member States to work across borders to combat transnational crime. President Obama announced at the U.S.-ASEAN Special Leaders Meeting at Sunnylands in February that we will engage all ASEAN members through our INTERPOL project over the next few years, beginning with the front-line countries of Malaysia, Indonesia, Thailand, and the Philippines.

Question for the Record Submitted to
Deputy Assistant Secretary W. Patrick Murphy
Representative Matt Salmon (#15)

Question:

In a July 2015 report, GAO recommended that the Bureau of Counterterrorism take steps to evaluate its efforts under its Countering Violent Extremism (CVE) program. Please comment on what steps CT Bureau has taken to evaluate its CVE program, specifically as it relates to efforts in Southeast Asia.

Answer:

CT evaluates programs through the use of objective, 3rd party professional evaluators with demonstrated technical capabilities in relevant law enforcement and security sector fields. These are competed either through the State Department evaluation contracting vehicle (known as the Evaluation IDIQ, or Indefinite Duration, Indefinite Quantity) or through wider competition conducted through government-wide contracting vehicles.

With regard to the GAO recommendation: CT has embraced the recommendation to evaluate CVE programming, and recently posted for competition a request for proposals for a process and program results evaluation, which will examine the process underpinning and supporting the development of projects, including the identification of drivers, the development of priorities and projects, and the program monitoring; and, a review of the results achieved, including what worked, and why projects were successful or unsuccessful.

CT has conducted large evaluations of the Foreign Emergency Support Team (FEST), Antiterrorism Assistance (ATA), Countering Violent Extremism (CVE), and Countering the Financing of Terrorism Finance (CTF) programs in order to confirm each program's role in the broader security sector assistance effort, to review accomplishments to date, better understand programmatic successes and failures, and to analyze the processes that over the years have guided programmatic decisions.

The results of these evaluations will have wide-ranging impacts, from refining programming to exploit successful approaches to revising both internal and external processes that have informed program design and strategy. The findings and recommendations from these evaluations will lead to more effective programs, more productive and analysis-driven processes, and more efficient management and execution.

Once evaluations have been completed, CT will be ideally positioned to take stock of progress made since becoming a standalone bureau, and to continue to build on the improvements made following the bureau's recent reorganization.

The ATA evaluation, which will be completed in early May, includes Indonesia as a case study country. The CVE evaluation will be awarded by the middle of May, and will include Indonesia as a case study country. Case study countries for subsequent evaluations have not been decided, but EAP countries remain high on the list of options because of the depth and breadth of CT assistance provided to the region.